THOUGHT-PROVOKING
PRINCIPLES FOR SUCCESS

JENNIFER L. BALDWIN

ABOUT THE AUTHOR

Jennifer L. Baldwin, is a passionate advocate for personal growth, leadership development, and lifelong learning. With a background in law, business, and personal development, Jennifer L. Baldwin has spent over a decade researching the principles of success and sharing this knowledge with individuals and organizations around the world. Drawing from both academic research and real-world experience, Jennifer L. Baldwin blends insightful strategies with practical advice to empower readers to unlock their potential and achieve their goals. Known for a down-to-earth approach and the ability to translate complex ideas into actionable steps, Jennifer L. Baldwin is committed to helping others define success on their own terms and pursue it with purpose. Whether through books, workshops, or speaking engagements, Jennifer L. Baldwin is dedicated to equipping people with the tools they need to navigate life's challenges and create meaningful, lasting success. To contact the author, visit www.jennbaldwin.com.

Copyright © 2024 Jennifer Baldwin

All rights reserved. No part of this publication may be reproduced, distributed, or transmitted in any form or by any means without the prior written permission of the publisher, except in the case of brief quotations embodied in articles and reviews.

ISBN: 9798330541898
Cover Designed and Published by JR Publishing, 2024

Dedication

To my family, for your unwavering support and belief in me. To my mentors, who taught me the value of growth and resilience.

And to every reader, may you find the inspiration to define your own success and pursue it with passion and purpose.

With love and light,

Jennifer L. Baldwin

Table of Contents

Introduction 1

Define Your Own Success 6

Embrace Lifelong Learning 11

Master Time Management 16

Build Resilience 21

Foster Meaningful Relationships. 27

Lead With Integrity 32

Stay Adaptable 37

Cultivate a Success Mindset. 42

Reference List 48

Introduction: Thought-Provoking Principles for Success

Success is a deeply personal and multifaceted concept, often defined by individual aspirations, values, and experiences. It is not merely about achieving specific milestones or acquiring material wealth, but rather about leading a fulfilling and meaningful life. In this book, "Thought-Provoking Principles for Success," we explore the foundational elements that contribute to a successful and balanced life, delving into timeless principles that have guided countless individuals toward their goals.

The journey to success is not a straight path. It is filled with challenges, opportunities, setbacks, and moments of triumph. What sets successful individuals apart is their mindset, resilience, adaptability, and the quality of their relationships. By understanding and embracing these principles, you can navigate the complexities of life with confidence and purpose.

Each chapter of this book is dedicated to a specific principle, offering insights, strategies, and practical advice to help you integrate these concepts into your daily life. From defining your own success to mastering time management, from building resilience to leading with integrity, these principles serve as a compass guiding you towards your goals.

Why This Book Matters

In an age of rapid change and constant information overload, finding clarity and direction can be challenging. This book aims to cut through the noise and provide you with actionable, thought-provoking principles that have stood the test of time. Whether you are at the beginning of your journey, seeking to redefine your path, or striving to reach new heights, these principles are designed to inspire and empower you.

The Structure of the Book

- **Chapter 1: Define Your Own Success:** Success starts with understanding what it means to you personally. This chapter helps you identify your values, set meaningful goals, and align your actions with your true aspirations.

- **Chapter 2: Embrace Lifelong Learning:** In a world that is constantly evolving, continuous learning is key. This chapter explores the importance of staying curious, seeking knowledge, and adapting to new challenges.
- **Chapter 3: Master Time Management:** Effective time management is crucial for productivity and balance. Learn strategies to prioritize tasks, avoid distractions, and make the most of your time.
- **Chapter 4: Build Resilience:** Resilience enables you to bounce back from setbacks and persevere in the face of adversity. Discover how to cultivate mental toughness and maintain a positive outlook.
- **Chapter 5: Foster Meaningful Relationships:** Strong relationships are essential for support and growth. This chapter provides insights into building and nurturing personal and professional connections.
- **Chapter 6: Lead with Integrity:** Integrity is the foundation of trustworthy and effective leadership. Learn how to lead

- with honesty, transparency, and ethical principles.
- **Chapter 7: Stay Adaptable:** Adaptability is vital in a rapidly changing world. Explore how to stay flexible, embrace change, and thrive in dynamic environments.
- **Chapter 8: Cultivate a Success Mindset:** A success mindset involves believing in your potential and maintaining a positive attitude. This chapter offers techniques to develop and sustain a mindset geared towards success.

Your Journey Begins Here

As you embark on this journey through the principles of success, keep an open mind and a willingness to reflect on your own experiences. Success is not a one-size-fits-all concept; it is a personal and evolving journey. Use this book as a guide to discover what success means to you and how you can achieve it in your own unique way.

Remember, the path to success is not solely about the destination but also about the growth, learning, and experiences along the way. Embrace these principles, apply them in your life, and watch as they transform your journey into one of purpose, fulfillment, and lasting success.

Welcome to "Thought-Provoking Principles for Success." Your journey towards a successful and meaningful life starts now.

Chapter 1: Define Your Own Success

1.1 Understanding Personal Success

Success is a deeply personal and unique concept. Society often presents a narrow definition of success, typically associated with wealth, status, or fame. However, true success is a reflection of one's values, passions, and personal aspirations.

Self-Reflection:

- **Identify Your Values:** What matters most to you? Values serve as the foundation for defining success. They guide your decisions, actions, and priorities. Take time to reflect on what you truly value, such as family, creativity, freedom, or contribution.
- **Discover Your Passions:** What activities make you feel most alive and engaged? Pursuing your passions can lead to a more fulfilling and meaningful life. Identify what excites you and how you can integrate those passions into your daily life.
- **Clarify Your Goals:** What do you want to achieve in life? Goals provide direction

and motivation. They give you something to strive for and help you measure progress. Reflect on both your short-term and long-term goals, and ensure they align with your values and passions.

Personal Definition of Success:

- **Create a Vision Statement:** Write a vision statement that encapsulates your definition of success. This statement should be a vivid description of your ideal life, encompassing your values, passions, and goals. Keep it somewhere visible to remind you of your purpose and direction.
- **Embrace Individuality:** Your definition of success may differ from others, and that's okay. Embrace your unique path and resist the urge to conform to societal expectations. Celebrate your individuality and stay true to what matters most to you.

1.2 Setting Meaningful Goals

Goals are the stepping stones to achieving your vision of success. They provide a clear roadmap and help you stay focused and motivated.

However, not all goals are created equal. To be truly effective, goals need to be meaningful and aligned with your personal definition of success.

SMART Goals:

- **Specific:** Clearly define what you want to achieve. Vague goals are difficult to measure and accomplish. Specific goals provide clarity and direction.
- **Measurable:** Establish criteria for measuring progress. This allows you to track your advancement and stay motivated.
- **Achievable:** Set realistic and attainable goals. While it's important to challenge yourself, setting unattainable goals can lead to frustration and burnout.
- **Relevant:** Ensure your goals are aligned with your values, passions, and vision of success. Irrelevant goals can distract you from what truly matters.
- **Time-bound:** Set a deadline for achieving your goals. This creates a sense of urgency and helps you stay on track.

Breaking Down Goals:

- **Long-term vs. Short-term:** Long-term goals provide a big-picture vision, while short-term goals are the immediate steps you need to take. Break down your long-term goals into smaller, manageable short-term goals. This makes the process less overwhelming and allows for incremental progress.
- **Action Plans:** Develop action plans for each goal. Outline the specific steps you need to take, the resources required, and potential obstacles. Action plans serve as a detailed roadmap, making it easier to stay focused and organized.

Regular Review and Adjustment:

- **Reflect and Assess:** Regularly review your goals and progress. Reflect on what is working and what isn't. Assess whether your goals are still aligned with your values, passions, and vision of success.
- **Be Flexible:** Life is dynamic, and circumstances can change. Be willing to adjust your goals and plans as needed.

Flexibility allows you to adapt to new opportunities and challenges while staying true to your overall vision.

Defining your own success is a deeply personal and empowering process. By understanding your values, passions, and goals, you can create a vision of success that resonates with you. Setting meaningful, SMART goals and regularly reviewing and adjusting them will keep you on track towards achieving your unique vision of success. Embrace your individuality, stay true to what matters most to you, and let your personal definition of success guide you on your journey.

Chapter 2: Embrace Lifelong Learning

Lifelong learning is an essential principle for achieving sustained success. It involves continually acquiring knowledge, skills, and experiences throughout your life. Embracing this mindset not only keeps you relevant in a constantly changing world but also fosters personal growth and fulfillment.

2.1 The Power of Curiosity

Curiosity is the driving force behind lifelong learning. It propels you to explore new ideas, ask questions, and seek out new experiences. Cultivating a curious mindset can open doors to endless opportunities and enhance your problem-solving abilities.

Cultivating Curiosity:

- **Ask Questions:** Never stop questioning the world around you. Ask why, how, and what if. This not only expands your understanding but also stimulates creative thinking.

- **Explore New Interests:** Step outside your comfort zone and explore unfamiliar fields. Whether it's learning a new language, picking up a musical instrument, or diving into a new hobby, exploring new interests can spark creativity and innovation.
- **Read Widely:** Reading exposes you to diverse perspectives and ideas. Make it a habit to read books, articles, and journals on a variety of topics. Challenge yourself to read genres or subjects outside of your usual preferences.

Embrace Challenges:

- **See Challenges as Opportunities:** Reframe challenges as opportunities to learn and grow. Each obstacle you encounter is a chance to develop new skills and gain valuable insights.
- **Learn from Mistakes:** Mistakes are an inevitable part of the learning process. Instead of fearing failure, view mistakes as learning opportunities. Analyze what went wrong, and use that knowledge to improve and move forward.

- **Persist Through Difficulties:** Persistence is key to overcoming challenges. Stay committed to your goals, even when the going gets tough. The determination to push through difficulties will strengthen your resilience and character.

2.2 Continuous Improvement

Adopting a mindset of continuous improvement is crucial for lifelong learning. It involves a commitment to ongoing personal and professional development, and a willingness to adapt and grow.

Adopt a Growth Mindset:

- **Believe in Your Potential:** Embrace the belief that your abilities and intelligence can be developed through effort and perseverance. This mindset empowers you to take on new challenges and continuously improve.
- **Embrace Feedback:** Constructive feedback is a valuable tool for growth. Seek feedback from mentors, peers, and

colleagues, and use it to identify areas for improvement. Be open to criticism and view it as an opportunity to learn.
- **Set Learning Goals:** Establish specific learning goals to guide your development. Whether it's mastering a new skill, gaining expertise in a particular area, or expanding your knowledge, setting learning goals provides direction and motivation.

Ongoing Personal and Professional Development:

- **Pursue Formal Education:** Consider enrolling in courses, workshops, or certification programs to enhance your skills and knowledge. Formal education provides structured learning and can open doors to new opportunities.
- **Engage in Informal Learning:** Informal learning can be just as valuable as formal education. Attend conferences, participate in webinars, join professional organizations, and engage in online communities to stay informed and connected.

- **Reflect on Experiences:** Regularly reflect on your experiences and lessons learned. Self-reflection helps you gain insights into your strengths, weaknesses, and areas for improvement. Keep a journal to document your thoughts, achievements, and growth.

Embracing lifelong learning is a transformative principle for achieving success. By cultivating curiosity, embracing challenges, and committing to continuous improvement, you can unlock your full potential and navigate the complexities of life with confidence and resilience. Lifelong learning not only keeps you relevant in an ever-changing world but also enriches your personal and professional journey. Remember, the pursuit of knowledge and growth is a lifelong endeavor—stay curious, stay committed, and never stop learning.

Chapter 3: Master Time Management

Effective time management is a cornerstone of success. It involves organizing and planning how to allocate your time between various activities to maximize productivity and achieve your goals. Mastering time management enables you to work smarter, not harder, and creates a balance between professional and personal life.

3.1 Prioritization Techniques

One of the key aspects of time management is prioritizing tasks. Not all tasks are of equal importance, and identifying which tasks to focus on can significantly enhance your productivity.

The Eisenhower Matrix:

- **Quadrant I: Urgent and Important:** Tasks that require immediate attention and have significant consequences if not completed. These tasks should be addressed first.
- **Quadrant II: Important but Not Urgent:** Tasks that are important for long-term success but do not require

immediate action. These should be scheduled and given adequate time.
- **Quadrant III: Urgent but Not Important:** Tasks that require immediate attention but do not contribute to long-term goals. These tasks should be minimized or delegated.
- **Quadrant IV: Not Urgent and Not Important:** Tasks that are neither urgent nor important. These activities should be limited or eliminated to avoid wasting time.

ABC Method:

- **A Tasks:** High-priority tasks that must be done. These tasks are crucial for achieving your main objectives.
- **B Tasks:** Important tasks that should be done but are not as critical as A tasks.
- **C Tasks:** Low-priority tasks that can be done if time allows. These tasks have minimal impact on your overall goals.

The Pareto Principle:

- **80/20 Rule:** This principle suggests that 80% of your results come from 20% of your efforts. Identify and focus on the 20% of tasks that contribute most to your success. This helps you allocate your time more effectively and prioritize high-impact activities.

3.2 Productivity Habits

Developing and maintaining productivity habits is essential for effective time management. These habits help you stay organized, focused, and efficient.

Establish Daily Routines:

- **Morning Routine:** Start your day with a consistent morning routine that sets a positive tone. Include activities like exercise, meditation, and planning your day.
- **Evening Routine:** End your day with an evening routine that helps you wind down and prepare for the next day. Reflect on

your achievements, plan for the next day, and ensure you get adequate rest.

Time Blocking:

- **Dedicated Time Slots:** Allocate specific time blocks for different tasks and activities. This helps you focus on one task at a time and reduces the likelihood of multitasking.
- **Buffer Time:** Include buffer time between tasks to account for unexpected interruptions and to transition smoothly between activities.

Pomodoro Technique:

- **Work in Intervals:** Break your work into intervals, typically 25 minutes, followed by a short break. This technique helps maintain focus and prevent burnout.
- **Regular Breaks:** Take regular breaks to rest and recharge. Use break time to stretch, take a walk, or engage in a relaxing activity.

Review and Adjust:

- **Weekly Review:** Set aside time each week to review your progress and adjust your plans. Reflect on what worked well and identify areas for improvement.
- **Flexibility:** Be adaptable and willing to adjust your schedule and priorities as needed. Flexibility allows you to respond to changing circumstances while staying on track with your goals.

Mastering time management is essential for achieving success and maintaining a balanced life. By prioritizing tasks, developing productivity habits, and regularly reviewing your progress, you can make the most of your time and work towards your goals efficiently. Remember, effective time management is not about doing more tasks, but about doing the right tasks at the right time. Embrace these strategies to take control of your time and pave the way for a successful and fulfilling life.

Chapter 4: Build Resilience

Resilience is the ability to bounce back from adversity, adapt to challenges, and keep moving forward despite setbacks. Building resilience is crucial for long-term success as it empowers you to navigate difficulties with strength and determination. This chapter explores strategies to cultivate resilience and develop mental toughness.

4.1 Embracing Adversity

Adversity is an inevitable part of life. How you respond to challenges can significantly impact your growth and success. Embracing adversity means viewing it as an opportunity to learn and grow rather than as a hindrance.

Reframe Setbacks:

- **Change Your Perspective:** Instead of seeing setbacks as failures, view them as learning experiences. Ask yourself what you can learn from the situation and how it can contribute to your personal growth.
- **Focus on What You Can Control:** Concentrate on the aspects of the

situation that you can influence. This empowers you to take proactive steps rather than feeling overwhelmed by circumstances beyond your control.

Develop Coping Strategies:

- **Stress Management:** Practice stress-reducing techniques such as deep breathing, meditation, and physical exercise. Managing stress effectively helps you stay calm and focused during challenging times.
- **Positive Self-Talk:** Replace negative thoughts with positive affirmations. Encourage yourself with statements like "I can handle this" or "I am capable of finding a solution."
- **Seek Support:** Don't hesitate to reach out to friends, family, or mentors for support. Talking about your challenges can provide new perspectives and emotional relief.

Learn from Failures:

- **Analyze Mistakes:** Reflect on what went wrong and identify the lessons learned.

- Understanding your mistakes helps you avoid repeating them and improves your decision-making skills.
- **Embrace a Growth Mindset:** Believe that you can develop and improve through effort and perseverance. This mindset encourages you to view failures as opportunities for growth rather than as reflections of your abilities.

4.2 Developing Mental Toughness

Mental toughness is the resilience of the mind. It involves staying strong and determined even in the face of adversity. Developing mental toughness requires cultivating certain attitudes and habits that enhance your psychological resilience.

Cultivate a Positive Mindset:

- **Practice Gratitude:** Regularly acknowledge and appreciate the positive aspects of your life. Gratitude shifts your focus away from negativity and fosters a positive outlook.

- **Visualize Success:** Use visualization techniques to imagine yourself overcoming challenges and achieving your goals. Visualization boosts your confidence and motivation.

Self-Discipline and Perseverance:

- **Set Clear Goals:** Clearly define your goals and create a plan to achieve them. Having a roadmap helps you stay focused and motivated.
- **Stay Committed:** Commit to your goals and persevere even when faced with obstacles. Remind yourself of your long-term vision and the reasons behind your goals.
- **Break Down Challenges:** Divide large challenges into smaller, manageable tasks. Tackling smaller tasks one at a time makes the overall challenge less daunting.

Surround Yourself with Supportive People:

- **Build a Strong Support Network:** Surround yourself with positive, supportive, and encouraging people. Their

support can provide strength and motivation during tough times.
- **Learn from Role Models:** Identify individuals who exemplify resilience and mental toughness. Learn from their experiences and strategies for overcoming adversity.

Adopt Healthy Habits:

- **Maintain Physical Health:** Regular exercise, a balanced diet, and adequate sleep are essential for overall well-being. Physical health directly impacts your mental and emotional resilience.
- **Practice Mindfulness:** Engage in mindfulness practices such as meditation, yoga, or deep breathing exercises. Mindfulness helps you stay present, reduce stress, and enhance emotional regulation.

Building resilience is a vital principle for achieving long-term success. By embracing adversity, developing mental toughness, and adopting healthy habits, you can enhance your ability to navigate challenges and bounce back from setbacks. Resilience is not about avoiding difficulties but about facing them with strength, determination, and a positive mindset. Cultivate resilience to empower yourself to overcome obstacles and continue progressing toward your goals.

Chapter 5: Foster Meaningful Relationships

Meaningful relationships are a cornerstone of personal and professional success. Building and nurturing connections with others not only enriches your life but also opens doors to opportunities, support, and personal growth. This chapter explores strategies to foster meaningful relationships both in your personal life and professional endeavors.

5.1 Networking with Purpose

Networking is about cultivating relationships with individuals who can provide support, guidance, and opportunities for mutual benefit. It involves proactive efforts to connect with others and build a strong professional network.

Build Genuine Connections:

- **Authenticity:** Be genuine and sincere in your interactions. Authenticity builds trust and fosters meaningful connections.
- **Active Listening:** Practice active listening by focusing on the speaker, asking clarifying questions, and showing

empathy. Listening attentively demonstrates respect and strengthens relationships.

Seek Mentors and Be a Mentor:

- **Find Mentors:** Identify individuals who have achieved success in your field or possess expertise you admire. Approach potential mentors respectfully and be clear about what you hope to learn from them.
- **Be a Mentor:** Share your knowledge and experiences with others who can benefit from your guidance. Mentoring not only helps others grow but also reinforces your own knowledge and skills.

Attend Networking Events:

- **Professional Organizations:** Join industry-related associations, attend conferences, and participate in networking events. These platforms provide opportunities to meet like-minded professionals and expand your network.
- **Online Networking:** Engage in online communities, forums, and social media

platforms relevant to your interests or profession. Participate in discussions, share insights, and connect with individuals who share your passions.

5.2 Personal Connections

Meaningful relationships extend beyond professional networks to include personal connections with friends, family, and peers. These relationships provide emotional support, companionship, and a sense of belonging.

Invest Time and Effort:

- **Quality Time:** Allocate time for meaningful interactions with loved ones. Whether it's sharing meals, engaging in activities together, or simply having heartfelt conversations, prioritize quality time.
- **Celebrate Milestones:** Acknowledge and celebrate important milestones and achievements in the lives of your friends and family. Celebrations strengthen bonds and create lasting memories.

Practice Empathy and Compassion:

- **Understanding Others:** Put yourself in others' shoes and strive to understand their perspectives, feelings, and experiences. Empathy builds deeper connections and fosters mutual respect.
- **Offer Support:** Be there for others during difficult times by offering emotional support, practical assistance, or simply being a compassionate listener.

Maintain Work-Life Balance:

- **Set Boundaries:** Establish boundaries between work and personal life to maintain a healthy balance. Prioritize time for relationships, self-care, and activities that bring you joy and fulfillment.
- **Disconnect:** Unplug from work-related tasks and technology during personal time. Being fully present in your interactions with others strengthens relationships and enhances your well-being.

Fostering meaningful relationships is essential for personal happiness, professional growth, and overall well-being. Whether building professional networks or nurturing personal connections, prioritize authenticity, active listening, and empathy. Invest time and effort in cultivating relationships that enrich your life and support your goals. Remember, meaningful relationships are a source of strength, support, and joy—nurture them with care and intention to create lasting bonds and achieve success in all areas of your life.

Chapter 6: Lead with Integrity

Integrity is the foundation of trustworthy and effective leadership. Leading with integrity means aligning your actions with ethical principles, demonstrating honesty, and consistently upholding moral values in all aspects of your life. This chapter explores the importance of integrity in leadership and strategies to cultivate it.

6.1 Ethical Leadership

Ethical leadership involves making decisions and taking actions based on a set of moral principles and values. It requires transparency, fairness, and accountability in your interactions with others.

Core Principles of Ethical Leadership:

- **Honesty and Transparency:** Communicate openly and honestly with transparency. Share information openly, even when it's difficult or uncomfortable.
- **Fairness and Justice:** Treat all individuals fairly and impartially. Make decisions based on merit and without bias or favoritism.

- **Accountability:** Take responsibility for your actions and decisions. Hold yourself and others accountable for their commitments and contributions.

Lead by Example:

- **Integrity in Actions:** Demonstrate integrity through your actions and behaviors. Be consistent in applying ethical principles in all situations, regardless of circumstances or pressures.
- **Respect and Dignity:** Show respect for the dignity, rights, and opinions of others. Create an inclusive and supportive environment where everyone feels valued and respected.

6.2 Servant Leadership

Servant leadership focuses on serving the needs of others and empowering them to reach their full potential. It emphasizes empathy, humility, and a commitment to the well-being of your team or community.

Prioritize the Needs of Others:

- **Empowerment:** Support and empower individuals to achieve their goals and develop their skills. Provide opportunities for growth and professional development.
- **Listening and Understanding:** Practice active listening and seek to understand the perspectives and concerns of those you lead. Foster an environment where everyone feels heard and valued.

Collaboration and Mutual Respect:

- **Collaborative Decision-Making:** Involve team members in decision-making processes and value their input. Encourage diverse viewpoints and ideas to foster innovation and creativity.
- **Mutual Respect:** Treat others with kindness, empathy, and fairness. Build trusting relationships based on mutual respect and genuine care for the well-being of others.

Create a Culture of Integrity:

- **Communicate Values:** Clearly articulate and reinforce the organization's values and ethical standards. Ensure that all team members understand and align with these principles.
- **Address Ethical Issues:** Address ethical dilemmas and concerns promptly and transparently. Encourage open dialogue and provide guidance on ethical decision-making.

Leading with integrity is not just about following rules or guidelines—it's about embodying ethical principles and demonstrating them through your actions and leadership style. By prioritizing honesty, fairness, accountability, and servant leadership, you can inspire trust, build strong relationships, and foster a positive organizational culture. Remember, integrity is the cornerstone of effective leadership and serves as a guiding light in making decisions that align with your values and contribute to the greater good. Lead with integrity, and you will not only earn respect and admiration but also create a lasting impact on those you lead and influence.

Chapter 7: Stay Adaptable

Adaptability is the ability to adjust to new conditions, challenges, and opportunities. In today's rapidly changing world, staying adaptable is essential for personal and professional success. This chapter explores the importance of adaptability and strategies to cultivate this valuable skill.

7.1 Embracing Change

Change is constant, and adaptability allows you to embrace and thrive in changing environments. It involves a mindset shift that enables you to see change as an opportunity for growth and innovation rather than a threat.

Mindset Shift:

- **Positive Outlook:** Maintain a positive attitude towards change. Embrace new ideas and perspectives, and view challenges as opportunities to learn and evolve.
- **Flexibility:** Be open to new ways of thinking and doing things. Adaptability

requires flexibility in adjusting your plans and approaches based on evolving circumstances.

Continuous Learning:

- **Stay Informed:** Keep yourself informed about industry trends, technological advancements, and global developments. Awareness of changes in your field allows you to anticipate and prepare for future challenges.
- **Seek Feedback:** Regularly seek feedback from colleagues, mentors, or peers. Feedback provides valuable insights and helps you identify areas where adaptation is needed.

7.2 Future-Proofing Your Skills

Future-proofing involves preparing yourself for future challenges and opportunities by developing relevant skills and capabilities. It ensures that you remain competitive and resilient in an ever-changing landscape.

Continuous Skill Development:

- **Identify Emerging Skills:** Research and identify skills that are becoming increasingly important in your industry or profession. Invest time and effort in acquiring or enhancing these skills.
- **Lifelong Learning:** Commit to lifelong learning and personal development. Take courses, attend workshops, and participate in training programs to stay ahead of the curve.

Adapt to New Technologies:

- **Embrace Technology:** Embrace new technologies and tools that can enhance your productivity and efficiency. Stay updated on technological advancements relevant to your field.
- **Digital Literacy:** Develop digital literacy skills necessary for navigating digital platforms, data analysis, and communication technologies.

Agility in Decision-Making:

- **Data-Informed Decisions:** Base your decisions on data and evidence rather than assumptions or habits. Analyze information quickly and adjust your strategies accordingly.
- **Iterative Approach:** Adopt an iterative approach to problem-solving and decision-making. Be willing to experiment, learn from outcomes, and make adjustments as needed.

Adaptability is a crucial skill that empowers you to thrive in an unpredictable and dynamic world. By embracing change, continuously learning, and future-proofing your skills, you can stay agile and responsive to evolving circumstances. Cultivate a mindset of flexibility, maintain a commitment to lifelong learning, and embrace new technologies and opportunities. Remember, adaptability is not just about reacting to change—it's about proactively preparing yourself to navigate challenges and seize new opportunities with confidence and resilience. Stay adaptable, and you will position yourself for sustained success and growth in both your personal and professional life.

Chapter 8: Cultivate a Success Mindset

A success mindset is the foundation upon which achievement and fulfillment are built. It encompasses beliefs, attitudes, and habits that empower you to pursue and attain your goals with determination and resilience. This chapter explores the key elements of a success mindset and strategies to cultivate it in your life.

8.1 Core Elements of a Success Mindset

Belief in Possibility:

- **Optimism:** Maintain a positive outlook on life and believe in your ability to overcome obstacles and achieve your goals.
- **Growth Mindset:** Embrace challenges as opportunities for growth and improvement. See setbacks as temporary and learn from them to enhance your skills and knowledge.

Goal Orientation:

- **Clarity of Goals:** Set clear, specific goals that align with your values and aspirations. Define both short-term and long-term objectives to guide your actions and measure progress.
- **Commitment:** Stay committed to your goals even when faced with challenges or setbacks. Develop a strong sense of determination and perseverance to see your goals through to completion.

8.2 Strategies to Cultivate a Success Mindset

Visualize Success:

- **Visualization:** Regularly visualize yourself achieving your goals and living your desired life. Visual imagery enhances motivation and reinforces your commitment to success.

Embrace Challenges:

- **Resilience:** Build resilience by embracing challenges and setbacks as opportunities for growth. Develop strategies to overcome obstacles and learn from experiences.

Continuous Learning:

- **Curiosity:** Cultivate a thirst for knowledge and continuous learning. Stay informed about developments in your field and seek opportunities for personal and professional growth.
- **Skill Development:** Identify and develop skills that are relevant to your goals and aspirations. Commit to lifelong learning and skill enhancement to stay competitive and adaptable.

Positive Self-Talk:

- **Affirmations:** Use positive affirmations to reinforce your belief in yourself and your abilities. Replace self-doubt with empowering statements that affirm your potential for success.

Seek Inspiration:

- **Role Models:** Identify and learn from successful individuals who inspire you. Study their habits, mindset, and strategies for achieving success.
- **Surround Yourself with Positivity:** Surround yourself with supportive and positive individuals who encourage and motivate you to pursue your goals.

8.3 Integrating a Success Mindset into Daily Life

Daily Habits:

- **Morning Routine:** Start your day with positive affirmations, goal-setting, and visualization exercises to set a productive tone for the day.
- **Time Management:** Practice effective time management to prioritize tasks, stay focused, and make progress towards your goals.

Reflection and Adjustment:

- **Self-Assessment:** Regularly assess your progress towards your goals and identify areas for improvement. Reflect on your achievements and celebrate milestones along the way.
- **Adaptability:** Remain flexible and adaptable in response to changing circumstances. Adjust your strategies and approaches as needed to stay on course towards achieving your goals.

Cultivating a success mindset is a transformative journey that empowers you to achieve your fullest potential and live a fulfilling life. By embracing optimism, setting clear goals, embracing challenges, and continuously learning and growing, you can cultivate a mindset that fosters success in all areas of your life. Develop positive habits, surround yourself with positivity, and maintain a commitment to personal development and goal achievement. Remember, success is not just about reaching the destination—it's about enjoying the journey, learning from experiences, and becoming the best version of yourself along the way. Cultivate a success mindset, and you will empower yourself to create the life you envision and deserve.

The principles identified in this book are interconnected and complementary, forming a holistic approach to personal and professional growth. By integrating these principles into your life, you empower yourself to overcome obstacles, seize opportunities, and create a life of purpose and fulfillment. Success is not a destination but a continuous journey of self-discovery and improvement. Embrace these principles, adapt them to your unique circumstances, and embark on your path to success with confidence and determination. Remember, the journey towards success is as enriching as the destination itself.

Reference List

1. Covey, S. R. (1989). *The 7 Habits of Highly Effective People: Powerful Lessons in Personal Change*. Simon & Schuster.
2. Dweck, C. S. (2006). *Mindset: The New Psychology of Success*. Random House.
3. Grant, A. M. (2013). *Give and Take: Why Helping Others Drives Our Success*. Penguin Books.
4. Newport, C. (2016). *Deep Work: Rules for Focused Success in a Distracted World*. Grand Central Publishing.
5. Duckworth, A. L. (2016). *Grit: The Power of Passion and Perseverance*. Scribner.
6. Brown, B. (2010). *The Gifts of Imperfection: Let Go of Who You Think You're Supposed to Be and Embrace Who You Are*. Hazelden Publishing.
7. Sinek, S. (2009). *Start with Why: How Great Leaders Inspire Everyone to Take Action*. Portfolio.
8. Maxwell, J. C. (2007). *The 21 Irrefutable Laws of Leadership: Follow Them and People Will Follow You*. Thomas Nelson.
9. Clear, J. (2018). *Atomic Habits: An Easy & Proven Way to Build Good Habits & Break Bad Ones*. Avery.

10. Pink, D. H. (2018). *Drive: The Surprising Truth About What Motivates Us*. Riverhead Books.

These references provide foundational insights and strategies related to personal development, leadership, productivity, and success. They have influenced the principles and strategies discussed in "Thought-Provoking Principles for Success," offering a comprehensive framework for achieving personal and professional growth.

www.ingramcontent.com/pod-product-compliance
Lightning Source LLC
LaVergne TN
LVHW061049070526
838201LV00074B/5231